EXPLORING WORLD CULTURES

Japan

Joanne Mattern

Cavendish
Square

New York

Published in 2019 by Cavendish Square Publishing, LLC
243 5th Avenue, Suite 136, New York, NY 10016

Copyright © 2019 by Cavendish Square Publishing, LLC

First Edition

Website: cavendishsq.com

This publication represents the opinions and views of the author based on his or her personal experience, knowledge, and
research. The information in this book serves as a general guide only. The author and publisher have used their best efforts
in preparing this book and disclaim liability rising directly or indirectly from the use and application of this book.

All websites were available and accurate when this book was sent to press.

Library of Congress Cataloging-in-Publication Data

Names: Mattern, Joanne, 1963- author.
Title: Japan / Joanne Mattern.
Description: First edition. | New York : Cavendish Square, 2019. |
Series: Exploring world cultures | Includes bibliographical references and index.
Identifiers: LCCN 2018015865 (print) | LCCN 2018017114 (ebook) |
ISBN 9781502643414 (ebook) | ISBN 9781502643407 (library bound) |
ISBN 9781502643384 (pbk.) | ISBN 9781502643391 (6 pack)
Subjects: LCSH: Japan--Juvenile literature.
Classification: LCC DS806 (ebook) | LCC DS806 .M384 2019 (print) | DDC 952--dc23
LC record available at https://lccn.loc.gov/2018015865

Editorial Director: David McNamara
Editor: Lauren Miller
Copy Editor: Nathan Heidelberger
Associate Art Director: Alan Sliwinski
Designer: Christina Shults
Production Coordinator: Karol Szymczuk
Photo Research: J8 Media

The photographs in this book are used by permission and through the courtesy of:
Cover Sozaijiten/Alamy Stock Photo; p. 5 yongyuan/iStock; p. 6 Rainer Lesniewski/Shutterstock.com; p. 7 Isao Kuroda/
amana images/Getty Images; p. 8 De Agostini Picture Library/Getty Images; p. 9, 26 Kyodo News/Getty Images; p.
10 Prime Minister of Japan/Wikimedia Commons/File:Shinzo Abe Official.jpg/CC BY-SA 4.0; p. 11 Guillermo Olaizola/
Shutterstock.com; p.12 Hiroyuki Nagaoka/Taxi Japan/Getty Images; p. 13 Chookiat K/Shutterstock.com; p. 14 1000 Words/
Shutterstock.com; p. 15 Pontafon/Wikimedia Commons/File:Tsushima Cat 001.jpg/CC BY-SA 3.0; p. 16 GCShutter/E+/
Getty Images; p. 18 artparadigm/Taxi Japan/Getty Images; p. 19 xavierarnau/iStock; p. 20 Christian Kober/robertharding/
Getty Images; p. 21 Diamonds/Wikimedia Commons/File:Reclining Buddha in Nanzoin Temple 20150429.jpg/CC BY-SA
4.0; p. 22 ikuyan/Thinkstock; p. 24 MasaoTaira/iStock; p. 27 Bob Krist/Corbis Documentary/Getty Images; p. 28 Milkos/
iStock; p. 29 muikrathok/iStock.

Printed in the United States of America

Contents

Introduction

Japan is a country in Asia. Japan is made up of thousands of islands. Most people live on the four largest islands. The country is long and narrow.

There are many mountains in Japan. Most of them are covered with forests. There are many volcanoes in Japan too.

More than 126 million people live in Japan. Almost all of them live in cities. Japanese cities are among the most crowded in the world. Tokyo is the capital city. It is the largest city in Japan.

People in Japan are close to their families. They work hard. They enjoy many sports and games. They eat delicious foods. They celebrate festivals and holidays. Japan has a long and interesting history. Let's learn more about this unique nation.

Mount Fuji rises over Tokyo, the capital city of Japan.

Japan covers 145,914 square miles (377,915 square kilometers). That is a little smaller than the US state of California. Japan is surrounded by the Pacific Ocean, the Sea of Japan, the East China Sea, and the Sea of Okhotsk. Russia is Japan's closest neighbor.

This map shows Japan's location and its neighbors.

Japan is made up of over six thousand islands. Most of these islands are very small.

FACT!

Mount Fuji is the tallest mountain in Japan. It is 12,389 feet (3,776 meters) tall.

The Ring of Fire

Japan is part of the Ring of Fire. This area of the world has many active volcanoes. There are 110 active volcanoes in Japan.

No one lives on them. Most people live on the four largest islands: Honshu, Hokkaido, Kyushu, and Shikoku.

Most of Japan is covered with mountains.

Tea is a popular drink in Japan. Here is a tea farm near Mount Fuji.

The Japanese Alps are the highest mountain range. These mountains are on the island of Honshu. Many of Japan's mountains are covered with thick forests.

People first came to Japan more than thirty thousand years ago. They **emigrated** from Asia. The first known society in Japan was the Jomon culture. Jomon people caught fish and hunted deer. Later they became rice farmers.

Emperor Meiji ruled Japan when it became very powerful.

For a long time, emperors ruled Japan. In the late 1800s and early 1900s, Japan became very

Japan's flag is white with a large red circle in the middle. The circle is a symbol for the sun.

powerful. During World War II, Japan bombed a US Navy base at Pearl Harbor in Hawaii. The United States declared war on Japan. The war ended in 1945 after the United States dropped atomic bombs on two Japanese cities.

After World War II, Japan changed. Public transportation improved. Factories were built to make different goods. Today, Japan is a world leader in trade.

The Fukushima nuclear plant was badly damaged in 2011.

Tsunami!

In 2011, a powerful earthquake and **tsunami** hit Japan. More than fifteen thousand people were killed.

Prime Minister Shinzo Abe in 2015

The emperor is the leader of Japan. He does not have any real power. Instead, the Japanese government is led by a prime minister and a **cabinet**.

Japan's government is divided into three parts: executive, legislative, and judicial. The prime minister is the head of the executive branch. This branch carries out the laws.

FACT!

Japan is divided into forty-seven sections. They are like states, but called prefectures.

10

The prime minister is chosen by Japan's **parliament**. The parliament is Japan's legislative branch. It is called the Diet. The Diet has two houses. They are the House of

The royal family lives in the Tokyo imperial palace.

Representatives and the House of Councillors. Japan's people vote for members of parliament.

The judicial branch decides legal matters. The highest court is the Supreme Court. It has fifteen judges. They are chosen by the cabinet.

A New Constitution

After World War II, Japan wrote a new **constitution**. It is modeled after the US Constitution.

The Economy

Technology is a big part of Japan's economy. The nation makes cars, smartphones, cameras, computers, and more. Well-known Japanese brands include Sony, Toyota, and Canon. Japan is also known for its traditional clothing. Kimonos are made by hand with colorful designs.

Girls wearing traditional and colorful kimonos.

Agriculture is important. Farmers grow rice, potatoes, vegetables, apples, wheat, and tea.

FACT!

Robotics is a big industry in Japan. Some robots can talk and learn new tasks.

A Yen for Money

Japanese money is called the yen. Yen can be paper money or coins. The paper money has pictures of important people from Japanese history.

Japanese yen are very colorful.

Fishing provides seafood like tuna, salmon, crabs, and shrimp.

About 70 percent of Japanese people work in the service industry. They work in stores, hotels, banks, and restaurants. They also work as teachers, lawyers, and as bus and train drivers.

Tourism is also important. Millions of people visit Japan each year.

Japan has many forests. Common trees include maples, cypresses, and beeches. Japan's most famous tree is the cherry tree. People come from around the world to see the beautiful pink blossoms every spring. There are even festivals to celebrate these pretty trees.

Cherry blossom trees line the path in a park.

Many animals live in Japan. Monkeys called macaques live on all of the main islands except

FACT!

Giant salamanders live in some of Japan's rivers and streams.

Hokkaido. They live the farthest north of all the monkeys in the world! Japan is also home to the Asiatic brown bear. They live everywhere, even near Japan's big cities!

Small animals include red foxes, sables, squirrels, and flying squirrels. Reptiles in Japan include many kinds of snake and turtle. Beautiful Japanese birds include colorful pheasants and cranes.

The Tsushima leopard cat lives on Japan's Tsushima Island.

Save the Cats!

Many mammals in Japan are endangered. The Iriomote cat and the Tsushima leopard cat are two of the rarest animals in Japan.

Most Japanese people are **descended** from ancient people who lived during the Jomon and Yayoi periods. A small percent of the population is descended from

Friends walk through a bamboo forest in Kyoto, Japan.

people from China or Korea. Others came from the Philippines, Indonesia, and Brazil.

FACT!

People in Japan live longer than anywhere else. The average Japanese person lives for more than eighty-five years.

The Ryukyuan People

The Ryukyu Islands were an independent nation until the 1600s. Now they are part of Japan. A minority group called the Ryukyuan people still lives on these islands.

A group called the Ainu are natives to Japan. In the past, Russia and Japan were closer together. Because of this, it is likely that the Ainu people came from Russia. Today, the Ainu are a minority. The Ainu mostly live in northern Hokkaido.

Almost all people in Japan live in cities. Japanese cities are very crowded. The streets are filled with people all day and all night.

Family is very important to the Japanese people.

Education is very important in Japan. Students start school when they are six years old. The law says they have to go to school for nine years. After that, almost all Japanese students go to high school. About half of them then go on to university. Students must pass a difficult exam to get into university.

Most Japanese families are small. Usually they only have one or two children. Men are expected to work hard to support their families. Many women also work. Others stay home to care for children or older relatives.

Cram Schools

In Japan, students must take exams to get into college. Many students go to special schools called cram schools for extra help.

Japanese students work hard on a lesson.

19

The main religions in Japan are Shinto and Buddhism. Shinto began in Japan thousands of years ago. Shinto says that there are many spirits called kami. Shinto rituals are done to offer prayers for good luck and positivity. Many people

A traditional gate leads to a Shinto shrine in Kyoto, Japan.

Europeans brought Christianity to Japan hundreds of years ago. At one time, the government banned Christianity. Today, about 2 percent of the population is Christian.

have a small Shinto **shrine** in their home. Others visit large shrines all over Japan.

Buddhism is another ancient religion. It started in India. Korean and Chinese immigrants brought it to Japan. Buddhists believe that a person's soul can come back to live many different lives.

This huge statue of Buddha is outside the Nanzoin Temple in Fukuoka.

Giant Buddhas

Japan has several giant statues of Buddha. One on the island of Kyushu is 134 feet (41 meters) long. Another large statue is the Great Buddha in Kamakura. Thousands of people visit these statues every year.

Language

Almost everyone in Japan speaks Japanese. Japanese is very hard to learn. Japanese writing does not use letters. Instead, it uses symbols called characters. There are thousands of different characters.

This student notebook shows Japanese characters.

There are three different kinds of characters in Japan. They are called kanji, hiragana, and

A person needs to know over three thousand characters just to read a Japanese newspaper!

Beautiful Writing

Calligraphy is the art of writing Japanese characters with a brush and ink. Children often learn this art in school.

katakana. Kanji were taken from Chinese writing. Hiragana are used to help write native Japanese words. Katakana are used to spell words from other countries. They are also used by most Japanese people for texting and emailing.

The Ainu people speak their own language. So do the people on the Ryukyu Islands. Hachijo is another ancient language. It is spoken on a few small islands.

Arts and Festivals

Japanese people celebrate many holidays. New Year's Day, or Shogatsu, is the biggest festival in Japan. It lasts for three days. People spend time with their family. They go to parades and eat special foods.

Lanterns float on the water during the Bon festival.

Bon is a Buddhist festival that is held in the summer. During Bon, people remember their **ancestors**. They decorate graves and leave

FACT!

Origami is a traditional art. People fold paper into animals or other shapes.

Colorful Books and Movies

Anime and manga are very popular in Japan. Manga are like comic books that tell stories. People around the world enjoy anime, or animated movies and TV shows. Hayao Miyazaki is the most famous Japanese anime filmmaker.

offerings of food and flowers there. People also light lanterns and send them out to sea.

Japanese festivals include traditional dances and music. Japanese people enjoy many kinds of music. Traditional musical instruments include drums and flutes. Rock and pop music are also popular.

Fun and Play

Sports are very popular in Japan. Baseball is the most popular sport. There are two different leagues, the Central League and the Pacific League. The Tokyo Giants are the most popular

Takahiro Norimoto is a popular player in Japan.

team. Several Japanese players have come to play in the United States.

Karate and judo are popular martial arts in Japan. Soccer, bowling, and swimming are other

Japan has hosted the Olympics three times. In 2020, Tokyo will hold the Summer Olympics.

Heavyweights

Sumo wrestling is a traditional Japanese sport. This sport is more than 1,500 years old. Wrestlers push, pull, and slap each other. Each wrestler tries to push the other out of the ring or knock him down.

Two sumo wrestlers face off during a match.

common sports. In northern Japan, where winters are cold and snowy, people also enjoy skiing and snowboarding.

Some people enjoy ikebana, or flower arranging. They create beautiful arrangements with different flowers. It is a relaxing hobby!

Food

Rice is the most common food in Japan. It is eaten at almost every meal. Sushi is also very popular. Sushi is made by wrapping rice and raw fish,

Sushi is a Japanese meal that is popular all over the world.

vegetables, or other foods in seaweed. There are many different kinds of sushi.

Japanese people also enjoy fruit and pickled vegetables. They eat many kinds of noodles. Soba noodles and udon noodles are very popular. So

FACT!

Japanese people drink tea at almost every meal.

Many Kinds of Sweets

Mochi is a popular, sweet dessert. Sticky rice is made into dough. Then the dough is stuffed with sweet bean paste or ice cream. The Japanese also enjoy pancakes and buns filled with sweet bean paste.

Mochi is a favorite snack or dessert.

is a tasty dish called ramen. Ramen includes long noodles served in soup. The dish can include vegetables, eggs, and meat. Dumplings are also popular. They can be filled with meat, vegetables, or seafood.

Glossary

ancestors   People who lived long ago.

cabinet   A group of advisors to the leader of a country.

constitution   A document that outlines the beliefs and laws of a nation.

descended   Related to someone who lived long ago.

emigrated   Left one place and settled in another.

parliament   A group of people elected to make laws.

shrine   A holy place that often includes objects or symbols.

tsunami   A huge sea wave caused by an earthquake.

Find Out More

Books

Bjorklund, Ruth. *Japan*. New York: Children's

Press, 2018.

Gitlin, Marty. *Country Profiles: Japan*. Minnetonka,

MN: Bellwether Media, 2018.

Kelly, Tracey. *The Culture and Recipes of Japan*.

New York: PowerKids Press, 2017.

Website

Japan

https://kids.nationalgeographic.com/explore/countries/

japan/#japan-gardens.jpg

Video

Japan Facts for Kids

https://www.youtube.com/watch?v=4jc8DP9K40A

Index

About the Author

Joanne Mattern is the author of more than 250 books, many for children. She specializes in writing nonfiction and has explored many different places in her writing. Her favorite topics include history, travel, sports, biography, and animals. Mattern lives in New York State with her husband, four children, and several pets.

Brooke

John Nael Friday

I WONDER IF
HERBIE'S HOME YET

I WONDER IF HERBIE'S HOME YET

WORDS BY MILDRED KANTROWITZ

PICTURES BY TONY DE LUNA

SMOKEY

HERBIE

LESTER

PARENTS' MAGAZINE PRESS/NEW YORK

for Susan and Amy

Hello…Mr. Franklin?
This is Smokey.
Is Herbie home?
He went skating…with Lester?
LESTER PINKNEY?
No, no message. 'bye.

Boy, that Herbie is one big fink!
That's a real friend.
A real NO-GOOD friend—
that's what Herbie is.
I mean what good is Saturday
if your best friend's not around?
Lester Pinkney...
Lester Pinkney just happens to be
the clumsiest kid on the block.
Lester Pinkney just happens to be
the smartest kid in the class.
I just don't happen to like
Lester Pinkney.

It couldn't be because of what happened
after school yesterday.
Couldn't be.
I mean I only said, "Herbie —
you're asking to borrow
the only thing I ever wanted
in my whole life.
My birthday present.
It's not even scratched up yet.
Ask me for anything else.
Ask me for anything else but my
new, red, high-rise banana bike."

He didn't ask me.
He just looked as I ran my hands
over those neat silver handle bars.
Then he said, "So long, Smokey,"
and walked away.
He didn't seem to be mad.
We didn't have a fight or anything
like that.
All he said was, "So long, Smokey."
It's like saying, "See you tomorrow."
Only you don't have to SAY it. That is,
if you're really good friends.

I'd give him anything else.
Anything else but my new
red banana bike.
Just last Saturday, we were sitting around,
doing nothing special,
and I asked him what we should do—
and Herbie said, "Eat."
And I said, "Like what?"
And he said, "Something sweet and cold."

So I got the dollar I had been saving
and we went down to CHARLIE'S.
We sat on the stools and ordered the
biggest, gooiest, ice-cream sundaes
you ever saw.
Then Herbie said, "O.K. if I pay you tomorrow?"
And I said, "My treat."
"You, Smokey Silver," he said, shaking my hand,
"are a great friend."
Then I said, "It's nothing. Forget it."
Well, he sure did!

Then how about the time
he was going away with his family
for the weekend.
There was Herbie, standing outside
my front door that Friday night.
Herbie, with the gerbil, the dog, the food,
the cage, the bed.
He didn't have to ask. I knew.
So I said, "Sure, I'll take care of them
for you. What's a best friend for?"
I remember saying, "Herbie, you forgot
to bring over the top to the cage."

I remember Herbie saying, "He'll never
make it over the top. He can't climb."
Well, he could. And he did.
Would you believe I spent
most of that Saturday tracking down
the gerbil?

And that dumb dog!
That dumb, homesick dog
kept barking and shivering—from
loneliness, I guess. I had to sleep
in the basement with him to keep him quiet.
When Herbie came home, he said, "I can
never repay you."
And I said, "It was nothing. Forget it."
And he sure must have!

I'll show him.
I'll take all my old comic books
and set up my own stand and
sell them all by myself and I'll
take the money and buy some new
comic books—and maybe some potato chips
and soda.
I'll get all the kids over and we'll
have a party right here
on my front stoop
where Herbie can see us and
will HE be sorry!

Maybe there's a ball game
down at the park.
Maybe I'll "ump."
Maybe I'll catch.
Maybe I'll hit a home run.
Maybe Herbie will see me.
Herbie usually plays shortstop.
I never told him, but you know—
he's a pretty rotten shortstop.
I never told him, 'cause you don't
to your best friend. But now...

BUTTERFINGERS! Do you hear me, Herbie? BUTTERFINGERS!

"Hello, Smokey. Home from the dentist so soon?"

I look up. Herbie's mother!

"Dentist," I say. "What dentist?"

"Why, Herbie said you had a dental appointment this morning."

Holy cow!

I leave her standing there.

I take off and I'm running like Niagara Falls right down to the bottom of the hill.

Fifteen steps up.

RING THE BELL AND WALK IN.

So I do...right over to the lady

in white at the desk.

She knows I'm late.

I wish she wouldn't say it. She nods her head—
"You're late," she says, pointing to
the one empty seat.
"I forgot," I say. "Would you believe it?"
She nods her head and points to
the seat again.
She never says much. She just nods and points.
I sit and I wait and I
wonder if Herbie's home yet.

If I could call him, I'd say,
"Herbie, Lester Pinkney is ALL RIGHT!"
I'd say, "Herbie, you're a great shortstop."
I'd say, "You've got a great brain.
You never forget anything!"
I'd say, "Herbie, you can borrow my
bike, any time you like.
And for as long as you want it."
And he'd say, "You're great."
And I'd say, "It's nothing. Forget it."

I wonder if Herbie's home yet...

MILDRED KANTROWITZ is the author of *Maxie*, published by Parents' Magazine Press and selected as one of the best books of the year 1970 by the *School Library Journal*. Mrs. Kantrowitz studied painting and sculpture at Pratt Institute, the Art Students League, the Brooklyn Museum School and the New School. She has worked as an interior display designer and an assistant art director in publishing. Born in Brooklyn, she now lives in the historic Brooklyn Heights district with her husband and two daughters, Amy and Susan.

TONY DE LUNA has illustrated many picture books for young readers including *The Twelve Days of Christmas, Whose Little Red Jacket?* and *I Want to Be Little*. A native New Yorker, Mr. De Luna graduated from the College of the City of New York and studied art at Cooper Union. A collector as well as an artist, he owns over 500 old and rare books for children, plus some 2,500 comic books. He lives in Brooklyn with his collection and his wife and three children.